A SCARRED SMILE

Marretta Floyd

A Scarred Smile

ISBN: 978-0-578-78272-0

Contents

Prologue

The hardships that we face in our lives always shape us in one way or another. We either get stronger, or hide from the storms. We either plant our roots firm in the ground, or let the wind eliminate our existence.

It is all up to us. How we let the adversities guide us, and mold us, and shape us is all up to us. There is ease after every hardship, but that ease is defined by the actions we take, and the reactions we give to everything we experience and accept as fate.

No one promised us a happy life, or even an easier one. We were sent on earth to experience this world and wear those experiences as badges on our chest. We are here only to bid our time as best as we can and learn from everything we pass by along the way. It is these experiences that make us wise beyond our years and help us glide through life a little gracefully.

This book is going to be about all those experiences I had and the lessons I learned on my way. It is about the person I have become now and the people who helped me shape. It is also about the people who came into my life to bring nothing other than misery in my life and how I tackled that phase. It is about how I cope with everything I wasn't supposed to cope with but what had been predestined for me.

You are going to embark on a rollercoaster of emotions. Some pages might make you cry. Some might give you an insight into my life. I do not promise a happy ending, but I do promise you a ride worth taking. I am Marretta Floyd, and this is my story.

Chapter One

Born out of Sin

I was born on October 10th, 1977, out of wedlock and into sin. My mom started tricking very early, and had lots of men. She chose to party so much that her kids lived without seeing her often. My mom would drop by as I remember to sometimes bring food and clothes and then be back on her merry way until I see her next time, and sometimes next time would be a long time.

My mom didn't only sell pussy, she sold drugs, robbed, stole and did whatever to survive at such young age. She was the kind of woman who would do anything to survive, but she didn't have much time for her kids because she was still just a kid herself. I grew up thinking my dad who raised me, was my biological father, but later in life I was told another man was my dad. It was never proven who really was. I and my two younger brothers still, to this day, don't know our real fathers because my mom was so recklessly trying to make it on the streets at a young age until one day HIV came knocking at her doorstep.

Everything that I am at this point of my life and what I know is because I learned from my grandmother and dad to be better. But, I still loved my mom and her absence didn't matter. My grandma taught me how to cut patterns and use a sewing machine. I learned how to sow seeds in the soil and take care of the produce, pick carrots and greens. She taught me to respect others. Marretta was called Retta by everyone while her dad and his mom had nicknamed her Piggy out of love.

My father's name was Rudolph Mitt Floyd and everyone knew him as Big Moose. My dad and my grandmother showed me nothing but unconditional love. My dad loved my three other siblings that he did not father, and often spent time with us all so we could be together at times when we were young kids. My mother wasn't ready for parenting I assumed at such young age, and then the drugs and alcohol use came into play which really made her not be around very often when we were kids.

When my grandmother would take me to church and teach me how to pray, I would always ask God to make me better than my mom when I have kids. I remember how my dad would sometimes fix my hair for church and school, and my grandmother would hot comb my hair. He would comb my hair and make different hairstyles and would do everything a mother is supposed to do for her daughter.

But my happiness was short-lived. Soon after I turned eight, my father was arrested for murder charges. He had shot and killed a man. I was just confused that the policemen were taking my dad to jail and why I had to leave my father's house and go live with my mother. I did not know what had happened until many years later. My father had a fight with another man over my mother and in his rage he killed that man.

Life hadn't been fair to me in many ways and fate had to intervene even when I had made peace about my mother's absence. I had stopped questioning her existence and importance in my life and had started to be content with everything that my father had given me. He loved me with all his heart and that was enough for me. He had become the center of my being and I was happy with him. And just when I became too attached with the feeling of contentment, life gave me reasons to be resentful.

My mother was the reason for what had happened and transpired between that man and my dad. I used to complain a lot to God because back then I couldn't understand a thing. The little humble and innocent girl Retta missed her dad who was behind bars and she only had her grandmother now in the whole wide world. But as children are forgetful little creatures, I soon started to find solace in my mother's arms. She was my very own beacon of peace now. She taught me many things and everything that I am now is because of things I witnessed at a young age.

I was only ten years old when my grandmother passed away. My dad was still in prison and there was no one I could share my pain with. I was left alone in this world again and this time I had to be strong for myself for whatever was to come next in my life. At a young age, I questioned God because I thought he had taken away my loved ones and was being mean to me and I didn't understand what was happening. It was the beginning of my years of long suffering, but I did not know it then.

Chapter Two

Exposed Too Early

He once happy and humble little Retta didn't have a clue that moving in with her mother wasn't going to be lovely and affectionate household she had seen living with her dad and grandma. I quickly learned that it was like day and night in between the two homes. I didn't feel that special bond and love from my mom. After moving in with Mom, I was sad to learn how kids could witness so much.

My mom held card games, her and her friends used drugs and alcohol and that was the time when I learned so many cuss words. I heard motherfucker and bitch more than I can explain. My mother was always on the go, out in the streets, but she kept food on the table and electricity on and we had our necessities. She provided financially, but as far as showing compassion to her kids was concerned, I don't believe she knew how to do that.

My mom was abusive physically, and sometimes, emotionally, and would get into fights with her longtime girlfriend. I and my siblings would always witness domestic violence of some sort even after my mom got married to a man, the domestic violence still went on as usual. The drug use went on till her very last day on earth. I don't recall a lot of very happy and joyous moments while living with my mom, but I still loved her dearly. It was more like what was going to happen today on a daily basis. Being a child or a teenage girl, you are supposed to have some of the happiest moments of your life, but I could never relate to it.

After moving in with my mother, I experienced everything that a child my age was not supposed to be even exposed to. I witnessed domestic violence, cursing, and alcohol abuse. You learn these things as you grow up and realize that it is bad. But, when you are a child, you do not know the difference between good and bad and you learn any and every thing including the things you were not supposed to learn. Children are great imitators and they imitate everything they see their parents do in front of them. I learned all the cuss words and profanity there was to learn from my mother.

I did not know that the man who actually raised me was not really my biological father. At least not until many years later when I was all grown up. My mother was still young and was had a different approach to life. She was still enjoying her life while leaving us at home, but I still loved her.

Chapter Three

Help Me!

While my mom was dealing with some very difficult times health-wise, my sister and I moved in with my mom's sister. It was tough for a while. In that small amount of time, I remember attending Campbell Drive Middle School. Going to school wasn't all happy and fun or normal in any way for me though like any other seventh grader. While living with my aunt, I was raped and assaulted sexually multiple times by my Aunt's boyfriend, Ronaldo Brian.

I was only twelve years old and did not know anything at all about sex, but was being treated like an animal daily. He would often say to me with pure malice lacing his tone that if I told anyone about things he did to me, no one would ever believe my word over his. I had nowhere to stay because my mom was sick and dying and he knew that which was why he kept abusing me and I couldn't do anything about it. He would always tell Ticker bell, my sister, to go ahead to the bus stop and say that he would take me to school himself.

I went to school with tissue balled up in my panties to catch the blood that would be coming out of my little vagina, because it couldn't accommodate him at all. My two little brothers did not live there with my aunt. It was just us sisters. I still cannot believe to this day how my aunt did not see how he treated me, and played with me and even how he used to look at me with his weird pedophilic eyes.

I had teachers at Campbell Drive who would constantly ask me questions like, Marretta why are you sad? Marretta, what is wrong? Why are you sitting in the back of the class? They just did not have any clue that I was being raped every morning while my aunt would be leaving for work. I was in so much pain, both physically as well as emotionally, but was too scared to say anything because I was being threatened every single day. He used to put a pillow over my head every morning while assaulting my body because I would cry and scream in excruciating pain. I was going through a lot at such young age and yet no one noticed what was wrong with me and how I was feeling. I couldn't utter a single word about any of it then because even though my dad was out of prison, drugs had consumed his life and my mom was dying, and I was just in a helpless state of sadness in my life.

Chapter Four

Forced to Grow Up Early

After being exposed to the most unthinkable and painful sexual abuse over and over again for an unimaginable time period, I was actually very happy to go back to live with my mom after she was doing a little better health-wise. But my happiness was short-lived.

In 1992, at the age of fifteen, I became pregnant, and shortly after, I had a miscarriage and lost the baby. I did not get enough time to mourn the loss because not long after I got pregnant again and gave birth to a baby boy on March 18th, 1993. I was only sixteen years old at that time.

When my son was almost two years of age, Mom took her final breath in the house we lived in. My sister was only seventeen while my two younger brothers were twelve and thirteen respectively. I still remember them playing in the basketball court when the ambulance arrived at our house because my mom was having some health complications.

I had been expelled from high school for taking a hand gun to school earlier, and because of that, I had to go attend an alternative school in order to get help with my son's daycare. I remember one of my teachers from the alternative school to this day, because she and I still share the same bond we did back then. As a matter of fact, Ms. Lodge was at my house when my mom left this world. She was the one who explained to me what code blue meant, because I didn't know at the time.

I remember her hugging me so tight with all her might and saying, "Marretta, she is gone."

Those words had struck me pretty bad as I started to cry uncontrollably. My mother wasn't the greatest mother when it came to parenting and showing affection. She even was very abusive and had beaten me countless times. She had been absent most of time in my life. She used to do drugs and sell her body. She had gave her life to the lord Jesus Christ before her final breath as I can recall a year earlier. But, she still was my mother. She was all I had left other than my baby boy and my siblings. And it was a sad state of affairs to lose even the little that you have left.

Chapter Five

Do or Die; Survival Mode

After my mom died, I immediately started to remember all the things I saw her do to survive. I focused on positive things because I vowed to never use drugs. So buying nice and expensive things such as clothes, shoes, bags, and household items like furniture, and basically anything you need to survive in this unpredictable world. I was only a sixteen year old teenager when I lost my mother, but I always was smarter than my age. I tried staying in school and take care of my son, and provide for my two little brothers, but it soon became too much of a load for me to handle.

My mom was on government housing and receiving SSI assistance, but because my sister and I were under eighteen, we were too young to receive my mother's section-8 voucher. So that is when survival mode kicked in for me because I was a sixteen year old dropout and jobless at the same time. I began dating older men to get money and the needs for me, my son, and my two little brothers. I remember trying to pull on a joint of weed and nearly choking on it. I never tried to smoke again.

I hated to fuck men for money, and I hated men at some point of my youth, I guess, because of the sexual abuse that I experienced earlier in my life. So, I started stealing food from grocery stores and clothes from department stores like Kmart, Ross TJ MAX, and anywhere I could get away with little by little, because my two baby brothers were still in school, and I promised myself that I would not allow DCF to take them away. Life was not easy for me at all, but my mindset was to survive at any cost and by all means necessary. I could not even get government assistance because DCF would have questioned where our mom was. So I stole food out of Winn Dixie daily and walked out of different stores with pampers, milk, and baby food for my baby boy. I was living an unstable life and had no help with the basic necessities of life because I remember my mom always saying if a nigger can't buy you a douche or a bar of soap you don't need them.

Made in the USA
Columbia, SC
29 October 2020